FRACTIONS OF LIGHT

M. Erez Kats

PublishAmerica
Baltimore

© 2007 by M. Erez Kats.
All rights reserved. No part of this book may be reproduced, stored in a retrieval system or transmitted in any form or by any means without the prior written permission of the publishers, except by a reviewer who may quote brief passages in a review to be printed in a newspaper, magazine or journal.

First printing

At the specific preference of the author, PublishAmerica allowed this work to remain exactly as the author intended, verbatim, without editorial input.

ISBN: 1-4241-6222-X
PUBLISHED BY PUBLISHAMERICA, LLLP
www.publishamerica.com
Baltimore

Printed in the United States of America

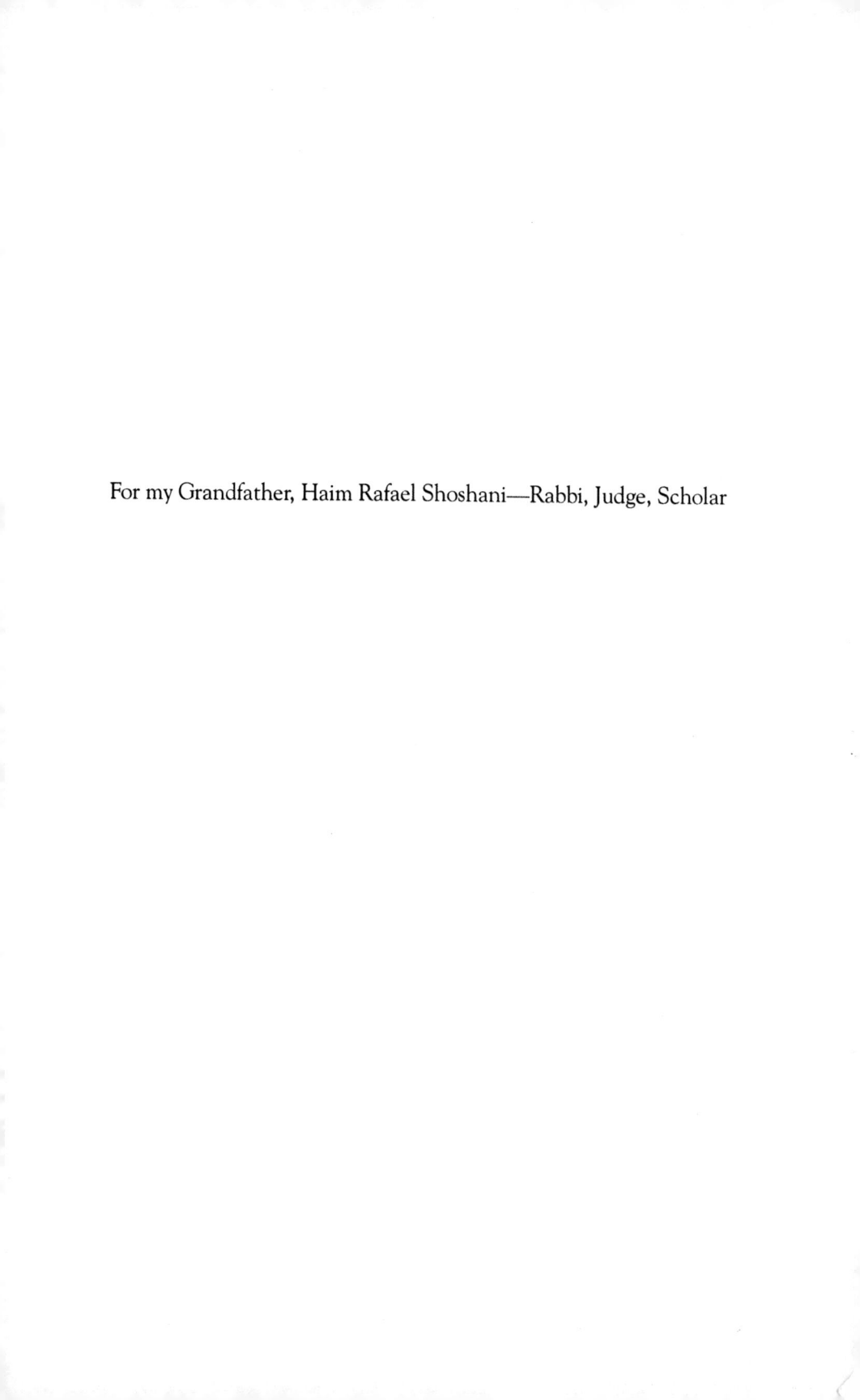

For my Grandfather, Haim Rafael Shoshani—Rabbi, Judge, Scholar

Special thanks to my mother and father, Bernhard and Ahuva Kats, without whom none of this would be possible. To my sister Ilana for continual support, and for instilling in me a deep appreciation of vocabulary, grammar, and the beauty of the written word. To all of my friends & family who helped me along the way. And of course, to all the girls I've loved before whom I will never forget!

DISTANT THUNDER

I lie in the dark with my shadows and demons close together
These shapes accompany the rustle of the trees in the humid weather
Time is no different, though it seems much too long
Events are no different, though something seems wrong

It's well past midnight, but I feel no urge to sleep
I am tempted to scream but I don't sound a peep
The body is restless and the mind is spinning
The heart is searching for a new beginning

Dreams of the future and past recollections
Are lost in a whirlpool of stronger affections
Thick clouds are above and the storm is approaching
I become very nervous despite repeated self- coaching

In the depths of confusion I can but wonder
About where and with whom lies the possibility of plunder
New images put me at ease and I'm weary in an instant
As my eyes slide shut with the crashing of the thunder…becoming distant

LIGHTS, CAMERA, FICTION

Again and again the public sends
Spies through the eyes of a camera lens
A few moments at random create heroes and goats
And we are taught to prize or reject their anecdotes

But one can't decipher the ignorant from the smart
When spectator and perpetrator are so far apart
Thoughts or actions from a scattered sample
Taken out of context as evidence cannot be considered ample

For a spontaneous decision does not reveal
How much a person should flaunt or conceal
To base a judgment or opinion on this it seems
Is unfair, presumptuous, and goes to extremes

So before we decide who needs to confess or redeem
It is we who must stop living a dream

VOICES

I love a sweet, gentle voice in the night

A smooth harmony that fills me with delight

Waves which penetrate further than sex

Currents that flow from ancient dialects

The warmth emanating while conversing so typical

The beauty of sound in voices reciprocal

Vibrations, electrifying my skin from every pore

Ebbing in and out like the tide at the sea shore

At night, in the fall, when the air becomes crisper

Morning, in the spring, with the breeze's cool whisper

Whistling and spinning in a faint murmur

Evolving into the deep chords of the baritone, much firmer

Who would have thought, the instrument in our tongue

Bursting from within, propelled by our lung

Too shy at the moment to shout, yell, or scream

When inside God's music trickles out through a stream

TIGHTROPE

I stood in the country and began to walk
The road became more and more narrow
The trees and the grass coming closer as they drifted away

The sun took shelter behind the snow-capped mountain peak
And the moon shined in broad daylight
Walking and walking the long, arduous road
Every time I came closer, everything seemed further away

Through deserts, fields, and meadows, through rain, snow, and hail
It seemed I'd crossed the world over
Rain sprinkling down in a white mist
The road grew narrow, and I could no longer see

As if I were walking through the clouds
The sky cleared and my shadow appeared
I kept walking until I had no strength left
As I was falling, cats came to me three

My shadow again vanished as I followed- 2 white, 1 black
As we moved closer everything seemed further away
The road was now so narrow, the cats trudged on in single file
Finally a cliff, separated from a forest by an ocean

The road narrowed to single rope, and the black cat spoke
"Your love and dreams await you in the forest, walk the tightrope so the ocean may not hurt you."

With each slow step, I saw only your face
On the final step you appeared from behind the tallest tree
You kissed me and held me, and gave me new life

HER

It was a dark, and very still night
Only a few stars and a light breeze
Events seemed to be carrying on in a similar replay
All the lights were blinking in the town, but the streets were empty
I stood alone at the lightpost, staring at the calm
I wasn't happy, not sad, just serene and content
At least I thought I was content
When suddenly a light and rhythmic click came tapping around the corner
And then…a vision…unlike any I had seen before
A sight that heated my blood upon contact with my eyes…
One that I could feel more than see
She glided around the corner, past the antique shop, with a soft arrogance
Light blue skirt twirled into her white tank top covering her tan upper body
I wasn't expecting it, but she stopped and smiled
Her teeth glimmering in the faded yellow of the street light
There was a star-like twinkle in her eyes with her head tilted slightly to one side
Her long blonde hair slid past her shoulders, and flowed midway down her back
She asked me with a sweet, cheerful voice if I would walk her home
Unable to say a word, I just smiled and started to walk
Walking next to her I felt on top of the world
A faint fragrance of roses emanated from her skin
Her hips, her whole body swayed so it seemed as though she was dancing
Finally, she stopped, and looked me straight in the eye
I watched her soft, pink lips as she leaned over to kiss me on the cheek
"Let's do this again sometime," she said smiling, before turning to walk away
I felt very touched, but could only stand there amazed and wondering
The rest, as they say…is herstory.

OUT OF THE DREAM

For as far as the eye could see, blades of forest green grass laid a carpet towards the distant future
Black marble stairs, piercing monuments, stone cathedrals to either side of me
The astonishing, omnipresent, overpowering beauty of man and nature all at my disposal
Yet all I could do was stare into the sun and dream
Insecurity and uncertainty were behind me, but something stood in my way
I could have remained here forever were it not for the mysteriousness of desire
My tense was future, but it contained a key
The paths of the past opened the door to the present for me

I knew not from where, but she appeared before my eyes
More striking and demure than I had ever seen or remembered her
She had a presence that was becoming of her, but was not her own
When I looked closely, I realized she was a reflection of myself
She was my past, present, and future desire all at once
"You have to stop sitting around and dreaming about me," she said
As I looked straight up at her immaculate body, I could not say a word
She walked elegantly over to a step on the fountain and sat down
"I'm going to sit here and wait for you to stop dreaming about me, just like you always waited for me when I needed you," she said and smiled
At that exact moment I heard the echoes inside myself
I awakened to what could, what should, and what would never be
I felt love in this strength, strength in this love
I took one step closer to the realization of what was once just a dream.

LOGICAL FLOW

We dance through life in a masquerade ball
Hunting for a feeling in a universal free-for-all
Some sailing, some soaring, some making bold statements
From war zones in the ghetto or after drinking in their basements
Life is just pinball and we hope we don't tilt
Each circumstance springs from one we just built
What's the adhesive? How do we hold it together?
Just one unit of mass to keep from drifting like a feather
Time makes all of us into shape shifters
Time is a caboose picking up all of the drifters
But we do have a gift that shows us a link
Alongside the motion is the ability to think
Then thought needs love to make it less aimless
Because like the devil, lady luck is not blameless
Escape misery, escape monotony, find the adventure
Search long and hard for your soul's thirst quencher
Curiosity has magnetic powers of attraction
Every man has the right to seek satisfaction
Continue to strive, to fight, and to cry
The pain will drown out and the pleasure magnify
The heart, the soul, the body, and the mind
We have the instruments…there's nothing we can't find

TENSION COMPREHENSION

There's a lot of stress in a world with no understanding
The tiniest details become so demanding

The cycle is wrong, it's spinning to a crash landing
Experience can be so raw and vivid, so branding

Because what you receive is not what you gave
To the game you fall helplessly a slave

A smile, a walk, a glance that's for always
Seems so foreign and impossible these days

Life's on a battlefield and you have to have guts
To reach a harmony, and escape the ruts

Kind of makes you wonder where it all went
Has the special time in life already been spent?

If one single kiss could communicate all
Then I'd be forever in grace and I could never fall

Make love…in the dark…with absolutely no sound
A silent vow making two to each other bound

That's the only thing that you could ever have found
The only way to keep your feet on the ground

Render yourself powerless with your every desire
Focus on one point and reach higher and higher

When a design so fine comes to mind
A humble existence…the only escape from the grind.

TEMPORARY ECHOES

I thought I heard you calling me
From the canyons of my soul
I thought the vibrations sang to only me
From the night, black as coal
I cried out for you
From the scorching heat of the desert
I thought that I could be heard by only you
And the sun cause no hazard
Every which way we dig down deep
Picking and picking at angles so steep
In the restless penetration, be careful not to fall
Each clump of dirt holds a grain so small
Each bit of grain contains the heart of it all
If you've sunk far enough, and can stand on solid ground
What's lost and what's found? Are you bound?
Is it dry? Have you drowned?
Can you measure it pound for pound?
If you can…let out a sound…like the howling of a hound
So deep down the earth isn't round…astounded!
Stop digging and sing! Stop falling, you're there
Listen to the echoes and you will hear her voice forever
But if you keep dropping…never.
Did she fool you? Can you call it a con?…maybe
Your choice makes the difference between temporary…and *contemporary*
No trust in the con, just as there's none in the contemporary
Forget it…trust her, trust life, trust yourself
In case you don't remember how…live for right now.

I SENSE WE KNOW EACH OTHER IN THE WATER

Sometimes the stickiness of the summer air swallows you
It gets hard to breathe, hard to think straight
Wide as the ocean, clear as the sky is blue
Water carries the coolness, and my senses stimulate

Movement is so easy, so carefree, so light
Burns, bruises, and scars, the wetness will soothe
Ballerina for the day, dance through the night
Current guides you along, pushes you smooth

Even more it performs with you and I
Each new warmth in the chill, a new connection
Strange ability to feel your skin with my eye
Glossy look, firmer touch, a magnificent reflection

With your pupils glistening, damp hair caressing your back
A beauty so natural, no hiding who you are
Colors burst with life, ending the slow fade to black
Soft as silk, mother's milk, you come from a star

Though our bodies grow colder, our passion burns hotter
Love…I sense we know each other in the water
Naked in unity, forever fresh
Cool, true remedy for the flesh

LONG AGO LONGING

I remember when time was magnetic…And all my energy was kinetic
Always laughing at the sun…Always the ability to turn and run
Tender innocence allowing me to bounce…Cat-quick, always ready to pounce
Now I'm beginning to wonder…
Was there something dangling at the end of that ball of string?
Was there really something to which I could cling?

They kept their distance, while I could not move an inch
Still half-asleep, still dreaming, I still haven't felt the pinch

I've seen love dancing in the clouds, swallowing my words
I know love's wisdom would render them absurd
Each and every time love's feeling sends me reeling
But here comes that western wind again, blowing on my back
Time to set sail…
Land ho! Yet nowhere in sight to call my own…
Nowhere to receive my mail

I remember when I knew what I wanted…before I knew so much
All the while wisdom keeps smiling…as this knowledge becomes a crutch
In the midst of this quest for belonging…
I sense a long ago longing
I want to see you again…want to see you again for the first time
Want to see you again for the first time, always
I want to see you again for the first time, always and forever

Standing here, I finally feel guided
At last this triangle is three-sided…but where?
The only time I have a sense of direction is when I don't know where I am
This need to find a place, I need to replace
This mystical, magical, wonderful place…I need only follow your face

Oh those ancient map-makers, who knows where their hearts went?
Oh those ancient conquerors…there could have been better time spent.

INFATUATION EVACUATION

If my life is any indication, my love is stuck in syndication

Total sexual suffocation, but I'm not one for vindication

I know I could fill her with elation, if allowed just one demonstration

Instead it seems I'm on probation, or that I've missed a calculation

I guess I'll go to the railroad station, and search for some appreciation

Travel around across the nation, embark upon a female exploration

Some must want some titilation…with no judge, no jury, no litigation

All it takes is the right combination, and love can burn in great conflagration

But all my experience and education, has led me no further than frustration

So I continue to wonder about a creation, who is mine beyond my imagination

This will forever be my inspiration, without a date of expiration

It's really quite a simple explanation, no need for a grand oration

But all of this endless contemplation, has left me with some constipation

So without any further hesitation, we may end this investigation

Because just when you think you've hit castration…

You realize there's always masturbation

APPLE OF MY EYE

The animals will tell you, just like the evening sun

Candlelit breathing of life and death, of those who believed what I do

Your eyes give me the light of travel, but I won't move further from you

I sit here in the dark, helpless, wishing for only you

Believe me I've known the models, with their elegant stride across the floor

Believe me I've sung with the lovers, who have danced in and out of my door

Still, the burning tenderness in your smile, and your lips made of human gold

Make life and a dream become one…In the only way my soul can be sold

In the only way I care to grow old…The only arms into which I can fold

In the only story I ever want told…the only way I wish to mold…this future

Let the water fall upon us, in the not too piercing heat of the desert snow…

In the not too sizzling freeze of the arctic soleil…

With all the sweetness of honey, the liquid dryness of wine so divine…

With the supernatural love that flows through me

Circular knowledge is the apple of my eye

Feeling that you'll always come back to me, leaves me not wondering why

Hoping that love can voyage, on a journey from one strong to one wise…

On a journey from one earthbound to one who flies

I refuse to call love confusion, because this fusion is no con

I refuse to relate love to fear, because then it may be gone

When I can kiss your hand as we lie in the sand…

Watch you sleep in the wind as it keeps you fanned…

When I can laugh at greed and fulfill your every need

I know I'll find much more love in me, and I know that I'll pray to the sea…

That there will be as much love in you, and that all your dreams will come true

Then together, as one, we can live…

And to the world, by our love, we can give

ESSENTIALLY BE MYSELF

Sensing what could essentially be my cell
Inside far too hard of a shell
I possess a true softness, but nobody sees
Other people's eyes seem like formal decrees
Their smiles feel like peace treaties
Leaving me with these desperate pleas, oh please!
Think my face is starting to display the weakness
My laughter is tainted with a newfound bleakness
For goodness sake, all this time and I finally feel fake
These images don't describe me, and I shake
Perchance this time is growing short
Perhaps these statements don't supply a retort
I feel no touch with no love, and I'm numb
I am deaf with no sound, and it's dumb
They spoke of the danger, to be happy and free
They said that we weren't meant for this destiny
I don't think there's any fault or blame
This crap is always the same
All this money and survival is their fable
Complete with their knights and their roundtable
Are we experiencing need or living greed?
What's the difference? They both make you bleed
I'd like to hang it all up on the shelf
See what should essentially be myself

CONJURE

Science has forsaken the natural mother who grieves
Magic has forgotten the delicate falling of the October leaves
Dreams have brought us to a madman who believes…
That love can be found if when he gives, he receives

Divine elation has her floating one level higher
Mortal frustration defeats him and he begins to tire
With the jury of inner peace, he wrestles with fire
She screams out, "Who is the subject of your desire?"
As his object loses its meaning, her ocean becomes dryer

Reality plays a mean trick, in this kingdom we see
Souls mix with time's ticks, in this quest to be free
Oh how he's been battered as he raises the white flag
His only true wish in life has a priceless name tag

Looking so thirsty, for an oasis in this desert mirage
Trying so hard to stay loose in this intense massage
In the pouring rain, she stumbles to a random phone booth
To resurrect his hope, to make it the truth
Simultaneously, they both cry out in spite of their youth

Conjure up that fairy, bring back my baby tooth!

PEOPLE AND YOUNG WOMEN

A wave of souls floats by us each day
Some young, some old, each beautiful in their own way
But we will only see what we can see
Time, and change, and nothing is for free

Embattlements go up in smoke
We feel like we're going to choke
While the good people lie awake at night
And, like most of us, they're out of sight…

No flaunting and no display, this has always been their way

They keep cutting while she tries
Taste her tears before she dies
Who needs truth if she lies
Who knows if we lost sight of her eyes

It'd be nice to make something plentiful…
With nothing to prove
It'd be nice to make something beautiful…
But the crowds don't approve

VIOLIN (for Papa)

I saw an old man crying, or was he flying
To a simple freedom stolen so early in life
One day his spirit took wings, or was it strings?
Miles and kilometers past the sea
Corner to corner, to beauty, to strife
In his heart, time is not counted in things
Another ocean leads to another garden tree…
That he planted, one seed beneath the trembling
One dignity behind the childish strength
Surgical cut beneath the length…of the scar
For which others have died, he has only cried
Finally a sound for you, and a new star
Blue sky and green grass grown from the wretched yellow
Perfection as only you know it
One note, one vibration, and indeed, the strings
Five voices, ten fingers, and the finest of things
The music protects us, carries us, guides us…
Penetrates the heart of us all
Pain, sorrow, happiness, and pleasure in its love
Every mischievous grin, every glass of gin, every supposed sin
Every meaningful win, every snowy inn, every silent wind,
Every time we begin, every place we've been…makes us kin
That old violin, baby blue eyes, and that violin

TIMBER WOLF (for Mamie)

Her eyes look through you
Her skin encompasses everything good and evil
Her nose knows all
Her beauty cannot be explained
Her spirit cannot be captured
Her will cannot be deterred…in this lifetime
Her innocence is her weapon
She hears everything
She fears nothing
She is herself, she is another
She is the black of night, she is completely white
She is every color in between, wrong or right
Near to death, she would fight this wild cat
For every last breath, to eliminate death
And in the impending gray…In the absence of night and day
The two of them in battle lay
To remain in light forever…For ties never to sever
Her shadow as light as a feather
This dog and this cat play together

LAST BEFORE FIRST

The outcome was shocking
The ends justify the means, what does that mean?
We may never know…
Because we may never realize when we get to the end
Our love happened before it was conceived
Relieved…it gives place to everything we believed
Power…we can't understand where it begins
Or if it continues until the end
All the way to the depths of the origin
You and I were always together, and now we are again
Timeless, when it's over before it started
A mystery, if you could make it all freeze
Motion came before movement
We were inside when everything was proven
Now we just keep turning inside
At the sight of my bride, nothing more to hide
Lost before I was found, or did you find that I was lost?
The line of fire has never been crossed
I am stuck inside of you…
Until these dreams can come true…
I will forever be stuck inside of you

A PLEA TO THE MAIDEN

In a world so distraught with absence
We are failing to capture the essence
The true force that touches us all…
And the time to let ourselves fall

Into the arms of the maiden
Who took us in from the start
So, on our happiness, blood and tears are laden
Strewn across every part

Oh God, how I've seen the fear in your eyes
The bitter tears in your eyes
I'd hate to think of your pain…
The lonely tears in vain

You see, to truly be a man
And do what few others can
Is to take her delicate hand
And observe where we began

While one more act of violence is killing that queen
And we can't see what has never been seen
My senses may not be very keen
But I'm as alone and angry as she must have been

Maiden, oh maiden, I'm praying, take me in
The outside world is the sin
Sometimes strong, but mostly confused
No armor against my heart being bruised

I need you inside of my being
Your way of feeling, your way of seeing
I've got to confess to this mess
And hope we can somehow be blessed

DEPTHS OF OUR SOULS

We may always be lost in the ever spiraling wind
We may be ever floating down some trail to our dreams
Some things may not be what they seem
Are we left to wonder which way the world has spun?
Or is there an answer to our newest desires
One more cannonball to be fired
Openness can only come from within
In our hearts, lies no place to end, no place to begin

Finally we've gone to explore the depths of our souls…
Where exists a new set of rules, and a very different goal
Something burning fiercer than hot coals
Where the actors portray entirely different roles
To walk down this path is a gamble, a roll of the dice
There's no telling if you'll be trapped in the ice
But if you can't trust yourself, who can you trust?
When we feel this inside, we do what we must
Memories become your new path home
Life starts to strive towards a golden dome
Trying to let your heart wear all of its jewels
But that's what makes us all fools…in this game with no rules

Wise fools nonetheless, because we know what we need
Indeed, your heart will bleed if it cannot feed
But for the seed to flower, it must first be freed
Of all the restrictions, we alone have created
Of all the convictions, that over time have grown faded
Let all the shadows and seasons fall at once
And let the trail grow wondrous again
The starlight night, the powder snow, and the morning dew
All laid out on a bed of roses, just for me and you

KINGDOM OF WISDOM

All you observe is all you don't know
All you deserve is all you forego
All of your time is all that you missed
All of your work is blurred in the mist
All that you want is all that is gone
All that you take is taken, like a pawn
All of your questions are all of your quizdom
All of your love is your kingdom of wisdom
In this kingdom of dreams, gods and goddesses are found…
immortal hearts are bound
In this kingdom of trickery, fools are clowned…while the rules make no sound
In this kingdom of justice, we weigh truth by the pound…
the earth is perfectly round
In this kingdom of elegance, the queen of beauty is crowned…she is silken gowned
In this kingdom of infinity, the clock is not wound

INSTANT OF FOREVER

One star shot across the sky
I caught it from the water looking up through my eye
Some kind of spirit, I know it was real
Something living in that water, Which I swear I could feel
Something living in my sweat, Piercing through my skin
It would not have come out, if it never was in
I've sensed your life in me, from the time of my birth
But for some mysterious reason, it exists outside of the earth
For a split second…an instant…it was there
I just happened to be lucky enough to stare
At the way completion must have looked
Amazed, at how easily this feeling had me hooked…
On the power of this universal plant
Which provides what all else can't…
Makes you feel as though you just might belong
As if there was a truth in the melody of this song
An instant of love, an instant of forever
An instant of a miraculous endeavor…
Which always was far too clever
To be imagined as real or dismissed as never…
She loved me that night from heaven on high
She kissed me from her sacred oasis in the sky

SWIMMING IN SILENCE

When I was a child,
I was perfect at the art of silence
Now I keep trying to convince myself that I exist
I keep living my life for a dream, a memory, a wish…
My imagination
But rainbows are only reflections of light, reflections of rain
You can't touch them…But somehow they always touch you
Will I always be affected by the weather? Perhaps…
But temperature is not the issue…neither is temperance
People will be what they will be, time will be much the same
And circumstance will dance around this game…
Is it a circle of fire?
Pushing you down into a dark freedom of spiraling desire
Or is it a flame?
Lifting your spirits higher than high…
One that will never burn you, or burn dry
Because we are all coated with holy water
And nothing or nobody can take that away
No matter how far our love goes astray
The answer is written on everyone's face
Finally…one day…we will all swim with grace

THE 8TH TEAR

In the tears of a mother, the whole world cries
The raping of innocence tells no lies
One tear is shed for the body, its spectacular force
Another falls for the mind, its endless discourse
The third trickles deep down, to the caverns of the soul
A fourth, the water spurting from a deep hole
Five tears for the air, bringing form to space and breath
Six tears touch fire, burning limitless death
But the seventh tear, is the one most desired
The easiest or hardest, depending on what's required
The one that unites *all* dreams and *all* tears
The one which conquers *all* pain and *all* fears
The tear that all of our hearts, wear like a glove
This tear of love, is white as a dove
The eighth tear is one that can seem very handsome
But don't be fooled, it holds life as its ransom
This, the tear that night steals from day
The tear that takes the seventh away
From the time I am born to the time that I die
Never shall the eighth tear I cry
In the arms of its mother, the baby sleeps tonight
Underneath the moonlight, everything is all right

THE LAST OF THE LONELY NIGHTS

Having sailed through oceans of time
Fighting the battles of my own confusion
Desperately grasping at the thickness of air
Feeling my soul tug at my heart
Fear and darkness looming around every corner
Catching a glimpse of myself
While the universe is painting the night sky
The answers are right where I left them
My pride is once again my guide

HALF MOON RISING

Tonight, I am half a man
Motion has stopped, and I no longer can…
Pretend that the waiting is for the best
Or feel that I should pass yet another test
I sense motivation must walk up hill
As the intense heat chisels against the iron will
Even if time is a mountain you climb…
The peak is where you can hear the bells chime
I look on the horizon, but no end in sight…
My perception is blinded by the beautiful light
So I walk with the elements, propelled by the earth
I am moved by the wisdom achieved after birth
Breathing air, drinking water, I now hold the fire…
But no control of my soul, only burning desire
So urgent to look deep into your eyes
Read the true chapter of where your heart lies
To understand why, and feel for what it cries
Together, our love will return us to the center
By your will and permission, into your life I may enter

SOUL INTENTIONS

I wish it didn't matter as much as it does
The best explanation may be "just because"

Some hours are much longer than others
This bond, as close as one between brothers

From these city streets…

I make superstitious wishes, I battle police sirens
Strange, how sometimes it burns, sometimes the fire ends

For the first time light seeps through the blindfold
It emanates hope, but the hope is still cold

We need confirmation to keep the flame burning
But the spark must come from a reciprocal yearning

Darkness robs you of far more than light
If happiness slips, you have to hold on so tight

Because this feeling shapes you more than your bones
Call it fear, call it hope…we can't be alone

The electricity of mind, the reunion of soul
Combined with the flesh is the ultimate goal

This sensation consumes you, it wears you like a glove
Evolve we must do, but invariably through love

ONLY ONE THING NEEDED

I wish I had the answer to all my questions
I want some facts, I'm sick of suggestions
Fear may dominate my only true need…
To conquer this may open my heart, but I continue to bleed
Opinions are as useless as directions
Because they don't seem to point towards our deepest affections
There's always a short-cut, an exit, a detour
Meanwhile, the precious moments grow fewer and fewer
Sometimes I feel I should drop everything
Strip down naked and forget the static cling…that grips me…
Like all the misguided, who don't understand…
Who think they hold my future in the palms of their hands
Because their whole lives they've been movers and shakers…
If one says no, there'll be plenty of other takers
It seems they never have time for themselves
Their lives aren't one of the books on their shelves
I guess we're all seeking out a few instructions
But they're nowhere to be found, so we turn to destruction
All we really need to find, is something that's real
Not merely what we want, but something we can feel

HEAR THE BELLS

Echoing tone from a far away place
Elegant figure dancing in her grace
Sunlight peering through dipping valleys
Blades of grass caressing cats in the alleys
Staring into the clouds, the form of a unicorn
From the wood and strings, melody is born
Ringing through the heavens, carrying a sound so bright
Piercing the void, from the darkness of night
Wildlife stirs with the coming of a new season
Warmth betrays winter, in a sharp treason
A nor'easter drifts through, giving us all a sign
Waves crash up and down the shoreline
The orange and red of the setting eastern sky
Flowering buds on the twigs, dignify
Thunder and lightning reek havoc in their wrath
Fluidity takes the form of all things in its path
Mais dans un seul moment…
Quand tous les choses sont sans movement…
You may listen beyond the capacity of your ear…
Bells, the beauty of music, you can hear

BASKETBALL

Hype has really changed the game I love
Not the players, but the media, has risen above
Same muscles, same grace, same desire to take it to the rack
But the lights and the camera print the game in black
There's something much deeper inside their hearts
Because teamwork requires work from all parts
A whistle, a foul, the sound of a swish
A high-flying slam or a last second wish
Bumping and grinding, down on the blocks
Thousands going crazy as the arena rocks
From the final seconds to the opening tip
Time, lives, and dreams count down a championship
No matter how much they ramble and analyze
The grace of the game still earns the prize
Despite the TV tension and pressure that mounts
It's still the ball, the rim, the player…
It's still the game that counts

REFLECTIONS

Whenever things happen that hurt you
Piercing thoughts that penetrate only a few

True care, true pain, true want to explain…
Feelings that move you to go insane

Words can't express the way that you feel…

It's written on your face in cold, hard steel
Such frustration when you wake up, and it's real

But this image only takes you as far as your heart
It dies a slow death, when the spectacle falls apart

How do you prove that you are worth while
When yours is just one, in an ocean of smiles?

The truth is something that has no bounds
It is a simple beauty, like a delicate sound

Critics arise from every corner of the street
Searching for a feeling, something concrete

What they don't know, is that it happens every day
And if you try to sum it up, in an instant of play…

You'll drown, you'll fail, you won't set sail
You'll have so many toxins you need to exhale

For pictures, like dreams, are rarely what they seem
It's the images that flow in a long, cool stream

Whether shadow or sunlight catches your eye
Reflections of love, can be heard in their cry

Time is my companion…
A single grain of sand in this colossal canyon

YOU

Your hair caresses your shoulders
Your eyes glisten in the dark
Your movement brings light to the shadows
Your smile decorates all sadness
Your voice gives silence a new sound
Your hands hold without touching
Your legs spring further than distant thunder
Your words chime beyond meaning
Your face transcends life itself

INSOMNIA

She wears her beauty with a silent elegance
In the garden of her so-called dirty dreams
Still, she finds her pleading heart alone…
She is frantically falling, praying for an edge to grab hold of
Lost…and desperately searching for that mortal angel…
He shall never sleep while she lies awake, crying

INFINITY

In this journey called life…
You're passing through time and experience
Memories stack up like a deck of cards,
And you can go anywhere in your mind
Because all you have felt and done…
Creates a mirror of yourself
Bending the reflected images,
Transforming your love into life
Into what you have always wanted,
Or everything you have ever wondered about
It could go on forever, there is no deception
You are simply trying the infinite perception

CASTLE IN DEEP

Live as magic
Fly cool wings to the moon
Happy castle dream of love
When sky is blue or stars yellow
As red butterfly follows my hand
Light a little time together
Destined for that fairy tale land
Melody is my silent vow
Until I can gaze straight through the sun

FUTURE CHILD

I can see everything I love turning to gold
I have found the secret passageway
I can see you have sent out your companion in beauty
I have found that you have raped her
I can see that true woman cannot be stolen
I have found that true child already has been
I can see where you are leading me

I can't see why you kill my time with your tears
I can't find my laughter
I can't see how you expect me to sleep at night
I can't find my dreams of the sun
I can't see what it is that's pressing on me
I can't find the points that need pressure
I can't see your face

But in the darkness, I see you transform light
And in the light, I find color
But in the colors, I find the red of my blood
And in the blood, I find liquid
But in the liquid, I find too much water
And in the water, I find thirst
But in the thirst, I drink your tears
And in your tears, I find solace
Sweet solace, I will comfort you…
And truth will return your youth
In peace we will reside
Our time, our love, our victory…will be the proof

BREATH OF THE RAINBOWS

It may be just a fantasy, you know
But I will search for one who glows
One who breathes the breath of the rainbows
An angel who swallows what she sees…
Placing it all in her heart
Absorbing, one by one, each of these…
All the colors of the light

Reasoning with the red of a rose at sunset
Originating under the rusted orange of the ancients
Yearning towards the yellow rays of sun
Giving as the green guarding masquerade of mother nature
Bearing beauty wide as the endless expanse of the blue sky
Intriguing, and inviting as the mystical indigo sea
Vibrating with the circular violet rhythm of music

In her movements, flicker all the changing shades
In her eyes, a twinkle, and no dimming grades
There are no rights and wrongs in her songs
Everything is one to her…everybody belongs

PURPLE AURA

The best inspiration comes when you are alone
Drifting in between insanity and hope, but still you understand yourself
It doesn't seem as if they have to, or if they ever will
False pity and guilt, transformed into illusions of you

They say that we emanate colors, that they're reflections of ourselves
Green if we're good, red if we're bad, yellow if we're in between
Do we shine or do we irritate? Exemplify or destroy?
Are we burning or glowing, in the twilight of our youth?

The victory lies deep in your heart, in spite of every defeat
Courage has to be visible, in some strange shape or form
Reminiscent of ancient warriors, rebels without a cause
The way they played is the way they lived, never managing to escape the storm

A beginning and an end, greets and departs us all
Memories and legacies, we have all heeded that call
To live for the future, or drown in the past
Is to drift at sea…without ever raising your mast

PITIFUL CIRCLE

In this world where nobody belongs
One thousand deaths could never be enough
Not even in one second
Thoughts of gloom have been replaced by impending doom
Hope…fluttering in the wind, as if hanging from a rope
We truly shall not win
For this time, we are rotten to the core
Sin, not powerful enough a word…
Not thoughtful enough an idea,
To save us from this disaster
Only time and shame
What a destination for this climb
Only slime and blame
What an explanation, for this crime
Another backwards cycle…in this pitiful circle

I UNDERSTAND

I understand why people die.
I understand why people kill.
I understand why I am dying.
I don't understand why people don't care.
What with all the crying.
We are all still nothing.
Not to each other, not to ourselves.
One long, empty, meaningless life…
A river of hatred…
Of each other, of ourselves.
We are all fake…like cardboard cutouts.
Without drive, without soul, without ambition.
We live in the dungeons of our nightmares…
Where we execute our dreams…
And survive…penniless, thoughtless, careless, heartless…
Soulless.
Money.
Death.
And a life without love…
Empty, fluttering, alone.

SADNESS

It comes when you no longer see God, or feel God
You cannot look in the mirror, for you are alone…
Your own worst enemy

Faith is little more than a dying dream
Love is nothing more than an evil scheme
Your potential has not been reached
Your soul has not been found

Sadder still when these gifts were once yours…
But they've vanished in the wind, washed up on the shores
You have lost yourself, lost your smile…
Another time, another place…you've lost the earth

And when it is all said and done…
Who will be the one, to return you to the sun?

It can hardly be you
So little that one man can do…
Against an army of strangers on hostile ground
FEAR, your only companion…
Creeping in, without a sound

PERFECT PERSPECTIVE

Appearance is cool, but no results
Your life needs a two-arm catapult
But why so quick to get where you're going?
Such a strong current against which you're rowing.

Too late to stop and too late to start
So many paths lead to so many different parts
And how are you expecting to turn out the best?
When you sit around idly as if you've been blessed.

It's never as easy as it once seemed
Reality is not quite as clear as you once dreamed
How can you work it from all the angles?
Sifting through and tripping in all the tangles.

Swimming through destiny without your goggles
Throw in a lover and damn your mind boggles!
Surely the fog will lift before midnight?
The opportune moment is within your sight.

Around the country, and the city you ride
Nothing else matters, this power's justified
Seemingly, there is some kind of answer?
Dancing with angels and necromancers.

Who knows how we'll be damaged or hurt
Everyone ends up buried in dirt
Statistics are wrong and statistics are true
But these violent habits and crimes stick to you like glue.

Sometimes just knowing that it's wrong
Can make you shy away and play the right song
Think, settle down, and you'll find the right action
Pump it through your heart and you'll get satisfaction.

Begin to comprehend how this time is different
Meaningful words are beyond coherent
Harmonizing, in its melodic true form
In the end can fill you up and take you by storm.

KNIGHTS OF THE NEW ROUNDTABLE AND THE ETERNAL LIGHT

KNIGHTS OF THE NEW ROUNDTABLE

The feast is prepared as the table is made
Sweet smells from the kitchen begin to cascade

The castle is filled with guests of honor
Chandeliers dim the light slightly bronzer

Candles pierce the dark and the light confesses
A secret mysticism twirling in the women's dresses

Butter, wine, and fruits stretch for miles
In a perfect rectangle like the floor's parquet tiles

Everyone laughs and talks about life
Do you care about love, do you want a wife?

New sight develops as you search for the one
Around her, everything rotates just like the sun

Neverending story, you wait for truth absolute
Will I ask the timeless question, is she really that cute?

True love is not a mere business transaction
Not political, no votes, no opposing faction

At this instant the stars are in motion
As you zip past friendship straight into devotion
Recalling the moment you cannot mistake
How you both felt that night on the lake

And then the day comes, she's taken you over
Got you barking like that ole dog Rover

She makes your heart sing, but did you do the right thing?
Are you eating table scraps, or food fit for a king?

ETERNAL LIGHT

What you give me I cannot describe
A perfectly soaring and beautiful vibe

Perhaps you don't know how much you are
But your very existence has carried me this far

My entire future is a reflection of your smile
We'll walk together until the very last mile

The sound of your voice sings to me
Inspiring me to believe and just "be"

Remembering the night when you washed my life white
Feeling you even though you were out of sight

Temptation has no strength against your blue eyes
Not a woman alive could unknot these ties

No substitution, no need for a fling
Just one thought of you can much more to me bring

Your elegance floats like that of a dove
From the earth below, you rise high above

Layer by layer, I keep peeling and peeling…
Stop the concealing and I'm drawn to one feeling

Searching for you, I need only but gaze in the sky
Time is no enemy, I have until I die

I will eternally sing this song
It can never be wrong…no, it can never be wrong

MAKE IT TIMELESS

They say only hope can be as strong as love
They say only the swan is more beautiful than the dove
But only because the swan, dances on water
It carries a knowledge beyond what they taught her

Elegance and grace, her only possessions
Fear and loneliness, her only confessions

Money does nothing for time's sacrifice
Selling out distributes the worst and highest price
If only our eyes could say more than our voice
If only our hearts would leave us no choice

The better off we'd be, the stronger we'd unite
The further from darkness, the closer to light

If I had it my way, I would kiss your tender lips
Connect with your body through warm finger tips
Searching, and pleading, and praying for a sign
That I am forever yours, and you are forever mine

We are all the same, and only love travels
Problems created and solved, as the dream unravels

Tell me a story of sun, wind, and rain
Tell me my efforts have not been in vain
On top of a mountain, at the bottom of the sea
In the gaze of an arctic husky, or the trunk of an old cedar tree

Make it timeless they say, and so does the swan
These moments are here today, but soon they will be gone

TEARDROPS

Don't let time and experience govern what you love
Let what you love lead you on through
They say the answer is three – body, mind, and soul
The force from the center, is the heart of the circle

Electric resonation flowing through your veins…
Can you feel what I feel? Have you the strength?
Life is but a function of love, perseverance but a function of time
Fitness leads to tranquility, the key – on your mark, get set, go!

Knights on your horses, raise your swords and coats of arms!
It's all in the choices you make…
Circumstances cannot bring you down
If I LIVE for you, I want you to LIVE…For me

In the end we're just teardrops falling from the clouds
In the end we're just teardrops drifting out to sea
In the end we're just teardrops saturating the earth
In the end we're just teardrops from our mother after birth

Yes, we are merely teardrops, no matter what we say
Tomorrow the teardrops of the past, will carry us away

WITH AND WITHOUT

Being with love, and being without
With love, all your best intentions just naturally come out
You're wanting to make someone happy, needing to see them smile
For them you would run every extra mile
You're worried when they feel sad or scared
You don't ever want their souls bared…

To a life without love, where everything is a game
Where they're always searching for angles, looking for blame
Ego is the building block for your castle
Everything comes easy here, and nothing is a hassle
Stuck in the pain of the past, you cannot find the suture…
Drowning out the present with thoughts of the future

You quickly find yourself lost and uneasy
Reaching for something, while you are turning it away
Slowly you realize that with or without…
Love is the only way

NEVER FOREVER

I do not want to hit the road again
Although the roads all lead to the same place
I do not want fall too far in
Although no hole is too deep
I do not want to break the ties
Although there are forces pulling me away
I do not want to forget your face
Although I can see it all the time
I do not want to see you cry
Although your laughter brings me tears of joy
I do not want life to lose its point
Although there never were any reasons
I do not want the mystery to be solved
Although sometimes I need some answers
I do not want things to get old
Although the new is missing something
I do not want to lose my spirit
Although adventure is disguised by time
I do not want to walk any further
Although my legs are not what is tired

I feel as though I've searched the world over
Although the earth is not my only one
I do not want this love to end, ever
Although my home is with you, home is never forever

CLEAR, COLD, AND QUIET

Not so summery of summer nights
A photograph has more motion
Crickets must have gone to Times Square
Frogs must have found their princesses
Halloween chill in this air
Waiting for someone, that is not alive

Poor howling hound barks at the moon
Everything you wonder about, no answers to be found
Oh silently…deafening, blinding, freezing…listless night
Vainly you're searching for the light
Will I be there when the sun rises?
Even a night like this carries surprises

TURNAROUND

It's time for a different taste
New outlook, new attitude, no haste

I can no longer see the danger in a stranger
The re-arranger of life in the heavenly manger

It has to be revealed, what I'm talking about
Thoughts without action carry no clout

Desperately looking through a maze of mirrors
Finding my reflection, my focus, and the direction of all my affection

People say you could only have won in the now
This I cannot comprehend as I wipe off my brow

From the desert, to the trees, to the drunkards I've traversed
But too often I find myself living in reverse

What a condition, I am young, but do I realize?
I wear clothes on the outside, but inside my cries

From this point forward, my will must be executed
The energy flows through, till I'm electrocuted

I shuffle through so many words, from the books on my shelf
If I just turn around, fear will soon be no part of myself

GREEN

Life is just a state of mind anyway
Why not make it green?
The grandfather clock is just a symbol
Of all we have seen

Building and building, but to what end?
Throwing away nature, how much it hurts…
The plants will lose strength, and even the rain will not mend
Nothing will replenish these valleys and their outskirts

Nothing to tear down, there's nothing to replace…
Soon we'll get our just desserts
In this deck of cards, we'll have used our last ace
Losing the warmth of the sun, the power of the universe…

Unless the blue sky is your mother, humble mother Earth
The green in her eyes, marks the time of our rebirth

WALK THE FINE LINE

They keep cutting while she tries
Taste her tears before she dies
Who cares about truth if she lies
Lost light if you ever lost sight of her eyes

Time passes & I don't laugh anymore
Muscles are working, but they shouldn't be sore
Pain is something they shouldn't feel
Love is now a feeling with no appeal

Be nice to make things wonderful
But the crowds just don't approve…
Be nice to find things plentiful
Without having so much to prove

I tried to give myself over to you
But you always failed to discover
Your beauty is a dream that actually came true
And that's why I became your lover

Maybe I have run out of gas…
Maybe I have lost all my class
But I know that I have spoken
And I know that the line is broken…

A survivor is all that remains

THE CHORD

The chord gets pulled
A million young ladies get lulled…
Court jester enters with his golden axe
Trust can't be earned without income tax

Now I realize you are the only one
I know it now, you are the sun
I'm free, I tried to make you free
I tried to make you see, there's no me with no we

I can't afford, to pull the chord
I can't touch your soul with my sword
The touch of your fingers, is what makes me so blue
You'll find no better friend, to get behind you

No sense of humor, for the broken peace of the dove
Chained up again, fallen prisoner to love.

THE GREAT LAKE

Intelligence not for sale
I don't go shooting at quails
Or chasing after long, dragging tails

Because what I know is just what I know
And I don't care about the rush, I have to take it slow
Only with time and temperance, can I truly grow

Forever caught between pleasure & pain
But I think I'd rather die, than go insane
Strength and courage, is what I stand to gain

At the one great lake, of my deepest desire
Where upon the water my name is written in fire…
On every heart, and in every head
And only the lovers will know what I said

GODDESS

This must be the end, my heart must be stopping
I want to cry, but I am already crying
Pain, hurt, fighting, anger…you take it all away
Nothing belongs to me now…I will do what you say
I'm on my knees, I'm on the floor
I kiss your feet, there's nothing more
You are everything, please stay with me
I love you my goddess, eternally

STARE

I won't take a break from you, or take a chance for you
I won't ache for you, or take a stance for you

I won't run from you, I won't love you
I won't gun for you, and I won't rise above you

I won't say a word, and I won't care
I won't change a thing, I'll simply stand & stare

ICE

Where did the sun go and why?
Is there a reason for this cold?
Does it possess a beauty of its own?
Or does it merely make us appreciate the warmth of flowing water?

So slippery here, I cannot stand
I imagine times of better balance
I like to feel the heat on my shoulders
Maybe everything is just nicer that way

But maybe my mind only catches things when they are frozen
Then I can store them in my heart keeping me warm
Instead of these wild images flying by me as usual
And gone too fast to suffice…
How odd that the river had to be ice

APPRENTICE

How will you use the knowledge they give you?

Organize thoughts to work in your favor
Pressure is not panic, but a moment to savor
Some of it is instinct, and some must be taught
Pay close attention and give things some thought

Make every test a personal conquest
Always stay one step ahead of the rest
Time makes us Olympians, fierce competitors
Keep body, mind, and soul intact from all predators

There are always some who talk, and some who know
Some who embellish, and some who show
Some who babble, and some who explain
Some who complain, and some who feel real pain

It's all in your personal perception
Not in the hear-say or phony preconception
The power lies inside you, clues are dropped on the way
What happens tomorrow stems from the actions of today

Finally you arrive at an understanding so true
Available to all, but earned by just a few
Love opens your eyes to the world of the living
When this vision is yours, you can truly start giving

IN THE NAME OF ALL THAT IS BEAUTIFUL

The sun cries out from the sky above
Giving the gift of warmth, sharing the touch of love
A cool, sweet breath blown by the breeze
Music chimes in from the rustling of trees

The birds sing about what they've always known
About the earth's rich soil, and the flowers that have grown
A mountain reaches up through the sky, till it pierces a cloud
Tidal waves pound the shore with thunderous crashes so loud

Rain sprinkles the earth with the water of life
Hurricanes roar in blowing their particular strife
But if you look closely, look the storm in the eye
You see that life's greatest gifts are given, you cannot buy

Yet still we persist in this torturous aim
And when we are stuck, we look for someone to blame
Of all that is beautiful, I cry out in the name
Open your eyes! And put an end to this game

I ARRIVE

Moving through spaces, every direction I turn
Each time I feel ready, there is more I must learn

I'll accept the passage of time, and I won't be discouraged
The closer I come to you, the more I feel nourished

From corner to corridor, always the unexpected
Memories and dreams, the same monument erected

My flesh and bones have become singers
They chant a musical power I hold in my fingers

Fingers stemming from the palms of my hands
When united with yours, we're transported to distant, beautiful lands

There's a fragile, tender point between hope and fear
It's tiny abstract reality can be contained in a tear

A billion tears in a million bottles, are floating in the oceans
Each bottle shatters on the rocks, pouring out a million emotions

I ponder why the salt of the sea burns your eyes
I wonder where on earth the mighty eagle flies

And although I now realize, this is the knowledge of kings
It takes some determination, exploration earns your wings

Still first and foremost, it's you I want to discover
Then together, above the world we can hover

Sail down every river, climb to every mountain peak
We inherit this love strong, and lift up the meek

FRAGMENT AND SLICE BY BLADE

The blade…piercing, slashing, cutting at the hearts of man
The samurai, with all his skill, has never tasted victory
Pointless labor forces him to sweat out his soul, or is it his anger?
Losing all flow…his life sliced into fragments by blade

Watch the lawnmower walk back and forth to nowhere
The grass cries out…why??
The trees poke and prod as they try to give a warning
Insects, fluttering about purposely trying to distract him

"What right have you to interrupt our lives?"
"How are we hurting you? Disturbing you?"
"We have always been your friends, your salvation!"
"And this is how you repay us…by taking our oxygen?"

We always think we have a better way
The blade…piercing, slashing, and cutting every day
"Take that blade to your own throat, and see if you can survive…
See if anything will ever grow on this land!"

It's time to go back to the ocean
It's time to observe the motion
Watch the water on the shore, and just study the flow
No slicing into fragments, just let things grow

THE PATH TO YOU

Winding, twisting, turning down the rocky road
So many sharp corners at high speeds
Inertia has propelled me any which way
I've had to hold on just to keep my control

As I finally reached a straight-away, the fog rolled in
A fog so thick, I wondered if I'd ever be able to see
Indeed, it was time for me to get out and walk
I was used to the rain, but not like this

Raindrops containing sunlight inside
Caused flowers to bloom inside of me
Drenched me with this feeling, and my laughter began searching
Under every table, in every dark closet, behind every curtain

But it's impossible to see inside a stranger
Until I pull the blinds on the blind man's eyes
Shoot an arrow deep into my heart
Until the internal bleeding starts retreating

And everything begins to flow as Tigris to Euphrates
Oh, how I've prayed it would happen overnight
But time stands still until you smile again
For I recognized your beauty…true and absolute

Head swollen, shaking and trembling, spinning round in circles
Put the thinking to rest, for I knew what I had to do
All fear aside, I could truly see your face
Someone said you were glowing

I smiled feeling the whole world feeling you
Gazed into your eyes, breathed your breath
There was no such thing as death
For the trail is long and beautiful

Come, we'll find our way to the cascades…
The rainbows, the waterfalls…The forests and deserts
The mountains, the rivers…every second, every day
Hand in hand, bodies tanned…we'll lie in the sand

DAYS OF CHOCOLATE

Being with you is a trip to the candy store
A chocolate bar for everything you are

You give me a fix better than a Twix
You tell me truth as innocent as Baby Ruth
You put the Joy in my Almonds
You carry me across the Milky Way
Your touch is Butter on my Finger
Your heart is thicker than a Snickers
What I'm really trying to say is Whatchamakalit?

All the chocolate in the world is not as sweet as you

FEAR

I stand before you…I am afraid
In your eyes the path has been laid

Are you blindly seeking salvation outside of yourself?
On your tippie-toes, reaching for what's too high on the shelf

Once again, something has slithered out of your grasp
More impossible to hold, the harder you clasp

Do you not know, you shall have what you should?
God would freely allow it, if only you would

But it's not that simple, and it's not that complex
Slowly his sack thickens, the more he collects

"I'll be seeing those eyes in my nightmares"
"Hearing that voice behind the blank stares"

"This fight…is blacker than night"
"This war…is not worth fighting for"

"Don't hide…let me see your true face"
"This is not black and white…this is not a race"

"I don't need to run…I know the meaning of one"
"I feel you don't scare me…when it's all said and done"

PROPHET SPEAKS FOR NO PROFIT

People always talking about the green, paper is all it is
Seems harmless enough, but here comes the vicious hate

Possession, what's mine and what's yours…
What does it matter? I'll give you what I can

There's got to be a point to these lives spent in pleasure and pain
Guess again…they're killing what's good, replacing what's real

Draining enough energy for the longest marathon
Time is not always this hard, don't doubt it

Let's give back what we can, lets try to understand
We're reaching for something that is not there

We're falling down a bottomless pit…
We're driving down an endless road …

She'll show it to you all, but where is she and why?
I've looked for so long, so many painful thoughts

She's inside of you, but you've got to dig deep
More and more, you know where you're going

Push it out and take a good look
No price on your life, no price on your soul

Everyone should have enough cash to share
But the almighty buck and lady luck dance together

Forget about it…money does not define your heart
The man who knows love, knows the woman in his mind

In him you can trust, we are one in the same
He knows your fears, doesn't want your tears

No price on your love, no price on your heart
Holding on tight, he will carry you home

I KNOW NOTHING

It must be possible…not to learn
To lose the ability to discern…
Whether or not to touch the dying fern…
Or the hot stove and know the burn

…is coming

Even deeper attempts to feel…
Although I know that they are real…
Leave me wishing for my tears
Faintly grasping for those years

…that are gone

If knowledge and pain isn't beauty…
Diamonds and pearls aren't booty
Peaches and cherries aren't fruity…
Man and womankind are not my duty

…is that selfish?

Love is all I ever wanted, all I ever need
Sadly that's been mistaken for greed
A beautiful face, a wonderful place
Turned to failure and disgrace

…and I know nothing.

THE GREATEST CRIME

They took my soul from me…
Expected me to smile
They took my vision from me…
Left me with no future
They took my heart from me…
Expected me to try
They took my life from me…
Left me with nothing

There is no action now…
Only time still to pass
There is no reaction now…
Neither positive, nor negative
There is no passion now…
No reversals of fortune
There is nothing left now…
Only ashes on the grass

Another love, another face…
They can't touch my soul
Another hope, another sight…
My vision remains clear
Another game, another race…
They can't kill my goal
Another day, another plight
I will always reappear

JEALOUSY

Envy is a cruel joke
Distorted fiction of the mind
Belief with no substance
The most pitiful grind

Sad, base self-consciousness
Sickness of the soul
A most pathetic hatred
Jealousy takes its toll

Total loss of understanding
Inciting dangerous reaction
Deathly love killer
Leaving no satisfaction

This cannot exist
In the purified heart
Feeling there's something you missed
Is not the place to start

DUTY

It's your duty to understand beauty
That every human heart does hold
It's your duty to understand the moody
Make them fight through life, not fold
It's your duty to understand the sooty
Because under this filth lies gold

It's your duty to understand beauty
What and why people need
It's your duty to understand beauty
We're all planted from the same seed
It's your duty to understand beauty
In every race, color, or creed
It's your duty to understand beauty
The only sweet form of greed
It's your duty to understand beauty
You see where it can lead
Love springs from mutual duty and beauty
Finally, you are truly freed

ENDLESS

When you're on that eternal journey
Passing through time and experience
Memories stacking up like a deck of cards…
And your mind can take you anywhere

Because all you've felt and all you've done
Are a mirror of yourself
Bending the reflected images…
And transforming your love into life…

Into what you've always wished for
Without deception, it goes on forever…
It's everything you've wondered about
As you realize you're trying the infinite perception

LOST NATURE

Not to be found in the city
The ability to dream…
A million souls fluttering about
Very few of them picking up steam

Some tainted, some fortunate
Demanding respect, while yearning for more
Too much and too little time
For what this day has in store

Confusion lurks around every corner
Beauty, a weapon of destruction…
Because sometimes it can be so rare
To find love without obstruction

In all this accelerated motion
Hearts are moving so slow…
Trying to catch up to what is passing by
Some starting to shrink, some starting to grow

A walk into nature is to stand in the center
As the world spins round your head…
You understand your place in it all
Why you are living, and why you are dead

And we find these places one by one
As we search for the healing hand
Looking down from a skyscraper, reaching for the sun
No longer those tiny specks in the sand

INSTANTS

Sometimes, for instance…
We laugh together through the truth
While remembering all the injustices…with a false sense of mercy
The power in that strength
To overcome the memories…as seen from the brink
Fortunes perfectly woven and given away…
As the world would like to think
Approved by all the evil spaces in the ivory night…
Against the sparkling day when he's fallen to his knees
The day he finally sees…
That everything is not what it seems…
But it still connects in our dreams

PUNCH THE CLOCK

It races past…
The greatest amount of time in which you could live
Shortened still by the absence of the love you could give
Stretched out for a period pre-planned
Timetable for the execs lying in the sand

They're tired, but what of?
Their every instinct and emotion could never approach love
They'll pull you and push you at full throttle
As they hold your precious time in a bottle

It's about the fastest, not the best way to think
But you'll never share their drink
Underneath it all lies a hidden layer
Where all dreams have died and everyone's stripped bare

Back to what the working man once called nature
Before all these robots, and foreign nomenclature
They're directing you towards your hard-earned death
Disposing of all their wasted breath

Deductive reasoning is at a loss
Corporate regulations are your boss
Kiss dreams goodbye as you once knew
Kiss life goodbye and all that was true

When all of these years have washed up on the shore
Your honest intentions have sunk to the floor
When the fruit of your labor is rotten to the core
And nothing is what you thought it was for

The sand in your hourglass is no more
And the broken pieces are swept out the door
Your life is now just modern folklore
As your strength slips away with the lion's last roar

EVERY DAY

Every day when I dream of paradise
Many others pay the ultimate price
Every day when I pray for peace
The souls of others are up for lease

Every day when I speak of love
Evil men say they've heard enough
Every day when I hope to kiss her
My lips turn into big blood blisters

Every day I try to be positive
So much harder when you're cognitive
Every day I look to the future
Mending these wounds with a new suture

Every day is beautiful
Every day is tragic
Every day is sinful
Every day is magic

Every day is bright
Every day is dark
Every day turns to night
Every day leaves a mark

Every day is success
Every day is failure
Every day is relaxation
Every day is revelation

But every day is just every day
Every day won't always find a way
Every day is the beginning of the end
Every day is the end of the beginning

TIME

Everyone's crazy and everyone's good
Everyone wants love and everyone should

But to look beyond, to forget the blame
To stand together to feel no shame

Life's black & white, but there's color in between
A rhythm from within, a flashy movie scene

Forget about all the blood, sweat, and tears
Traveler on a mission, companion to the years
A life of meaning, have a few beers

Time is just a mountain you climb
Time speaks just like a mime
But this silence is not a crime

Everything you want is everything you need
Time is the plant after the seed

In the desperation of time…
Just people and places we all must find

WAITING FOR A DISASTER

Hoping it will end before they lose themselves
As their eyes peer away from you

Can't let their love flow or let it show
As their smiles flash and fade like lightning

Fear hibernates in their soul
As the tiniest things loom so large

Summer turns to winter
Cupid's arrows turn to splinters

It's as if they're all waiting for a disaster
You see it as you walk right past her
The look in her eyes as her heart sinks faster and faster

SCATTERED UNIVERSE

The deepest trips, penetrations of the mind
Don't touch the soul as one would hope
What should be love is now work
How can you share this beauty?

If you can perfect it on paper, it may never be lost in time
But there remains no explanation
To lose yourself in it, is to become blind
Even if only for a moment

Your sight drifting aimlessly away from the paper
Into silence, then a sound, then a dream
To create the impossible is a possibility
But feelings must be projected

Universality is rhythm, perception is vision
No love is single, they all intermingle
Beyond is the flow, the touch, the connection
Beneath is destiny, human and divine

Needless to say there is accomplishment here
Struggles lead to celebrations, which is why you are living
Emotional transformation is what you are giving
All for the greater good

PERISH

Told me you'd testify to a higher power
Took it blindly, believing in pure gold
Someone of such truth does not exist
This purity I do not deserve

I'm a fool stumbling through a mine field
Seeing nothing with my sterling vision
My body contains just flesh
The spirit in my eyes is no longer fresh

I can't continue to desecrate others
With false pretenses of a love that cannot be
As I search through them, not for them
And find rich emptiness, not a soul's substance

When searching for nothing, that is what's found
Endless fluctuation leaves me alone
Everything I thought I cherished
I find has already has perished

BY THE SPIRIT UNVEIL

By the spirit unveil, the sharpest corner of your smile
If the spirit fail, your kindest heart reconcile

By the wind set sail, the blue-green salt water in your eyes
If the body's frail, let strength overcome size

By the darkest night, a star gives a year of its light
In the dangerous flight, venture well beyond fright

Your solid devotion, turn stone to ice
Your genuine emotion, the bubbling heat and the spice
Silver elegance floats, with movement so precise
Golden chalice your face, in love's very name will entice

I'll meet you in the galaxy, of destiny's secret vow
A milky way of time, the earth will allow
At the end of the journey, at your feet I will bow
But I won't wipe the sweat from my brow
Until I've learned how, until I know how

By the spirit unveil…my nakedness before you
By the spirit unveil…My fears forgotten for you
By the spirit unveil…my life and dreams before you
By the spirit unveil…My tears dropped for you

By the spirit inhale…another deep breath for you
By the spirit exhale…my death before you
By the spirit unveil…the skin, the body, the union
By the spirit unveil…my manhood in you

Your face and your name…
In the midst of the frozen black forest…
The flame

HOPING I'M OPENING UP FOR YOU

My best attempt at your endless drifting love
Is exposing my heart to the powers from above

Don't want roadblocks on this trail
Don't want my tiniest emotions to go stale

I feel as though I'm losing you, amidst all the fuss
In no one's eyes, can I find the light to trust…and discuss

Another new pattern on this drowning quilt
Everything is crumbling, all I thought I had built

No more sweet yesterdays, or tomorrows in grace
No solar rays, while I'm spiraling in space

Patience is supposed to be my best friend
But still I can see no end…to this

Time is my companion…
A grain of sand in this colossal canyon

Maybe the earth will swallow it up
Maybe the heavens will wash it away

Yet I still feel this presence from beyond
No clue, if these miles apart bring me closer to you

Believe me, I have the strength for that length
The devotion for that emotion
The pride to be by your side
The time to continue to climb
The heart to play my part
The soul to reach our goal
I have the love which you dream of

Now I need the prize of your eyes, to realize
Even in disguise, the size of compromise
That defies any lack of emotional ties
Hoping I'm opening up for you

DEEP-SEA MINING

Coming here is like a sewing machine
But I'm all out of string

Coming here is like a vaccine
But I don't feel the sting

Coming here is like a canteen
But there's no water to bring

Coming here is like every castle I've seen
But I cannot be the king

Coming here together, even through the weather
We'll be able to sing

Coming here…what does it mean?
Everything

Underneath my skin like a submarine
Torn in two, but I hear the bells ring

Coming here with the earth so green
Excavation like this is deep-sea mining

BABBLE ON

Who's to say circumstance is a game of chance?
If the shoe fits wear it, but don't try to compare it

Why do they call it a miracle?
Just because they've never seen it and can't explain it?
History will teach us nothing, but that's not where we live anyway

The flame may rise up through the mountains
Cloud the countryside with smoke
Rain can't cleanse the earth of it's dirt
Waves and rays will ultimately dig clear through to the destination

Sometimes love means forgetting about everything and making an offer
Can you truly guide time past this freeze frame?
The colors of a flag only display the differences of the territories…

And we all babble on…back to Babylon

CONCENTRIC CIRCLES

Roll with it, live your life this way
Good feelings and good hearts take you to another day
Get the power, find it right now
The $8 spin will make you say "wow!"

You see the light, in its full clarity
You shy away from all the insincerity
Reachin' common ground with your very best friend
Out of your soul lots of love to send

Top of Lee Circle lookin' out on the town
Getting' it off your chest and just moving around
Homeless people passed out in the courtyard
The remnants of a society that's scarred

Taking yourself and realizing your power
Will lead you to the light in your finest hour
Prepare…for the battle in the trenches
Armed with excitement, feel when your fist clenches

God drops his clues all over the earth
To see how we interpret them, see what we're worth
Incredible, miraculous, amazing it may be
But the real test is to find your own ecstasy

THE GOLDEN PATH

We all see each other
Shiny, lustrous diamonds in our hearts
Drifting and floating high above…
Over the mountain tops and city lights of our dreams
To that one central place…
Absent of disgrace in its vast, mystical space
And love…
High on a pedestal where it belongs.
Visionless, motionless, serene.
Such a kingdom for you and me, or she and he
And oceans…upon oceans…of treasures…and time

THE SANDBOX

I couldn't even tell…If I was a man or a woman
I didn't really know…That we weren't in the water
There may be wars going on all around us

But this, this is love…
The way love is supposed to be…

Tender and warm, silent and special
Juicy and wet, exciting and exasperating

Smiling eyes, a true feeling of unity

I can taste her body, want to drink her beauty
But swimming in this orgasmic moment, there is but one image I can see…

Two children in a sandbox…playing joyfully
Two hearts exploring, reaching for their destiny

A boy and a girl, a woman and a man
Couldn't tell where my body ended…or where hers began

PRETENDING

You wake up in a palace of broken dreams…
Shattered, by nightmares of the past
Fueled by desires of the present…
Rumbling in your heavy heart like thunder
Echoing through canyons of discontent and confusion.

A smile…once so natural…is now pretending
A far off land, a faint twinkling star…
Racing feverishly through your soul's dark ocean
A churning abyss, a bottomless chasm
Is there any goodness in this world?

Only by comparison, only through fate
One man's castle is another man's cauldron of hate
Melting, and bubbling into unknown riches
Yet we are one in the same, sharing equal fame…
Equal pain…dollars and flowers, pride and shame

We have not yet learned, our true plight
We have not to this day…abandoned the fight
The struggle, for that which we cannot resist
The vision, of that which does not exist
Only spirits…clashing and colliding…
And fading in the summer mist

BLIND

Everyone's got something to say…
Except what is wrong with my life?
When amidst all those material gains
Lie traces and echoes of strife

Among all of our children with badly scarred hearts
And all of our history torn violently apart

We have sought one moment in the sun
Through all of the thunder and the rain
Drenched painfully like our dreams…
Our lack of comprehension, our pain

Until all those sweet tales…
Of happiness gone by
Become artificial thoughts…
Seen through artificial eyes

No wonder we have been so unkind
No wonder we have proven, to be so blind

GRACE

If pain could be transformed into love…
It would be written on her face

If God lived somewhere in the air…
He would be taking up her space

If I ever looked into an eye…
That gave me permission to cry

I would weep for days…
In that auspicious gaze
Dreaming of an island
In this labyrinth, this maze

But we are not fated…
To live what we have not created

In a mind so trained…
To expect the rain

Or maybe just tainted…
And therefore sainted

I would weep for days…
In that auspicious gaze
Dreaming of an island
In this labyrinth, this maze

Sunshine, but a secret lie
Looming high up in the sky

A ball of pure fire…
Heats the desert sand dune

For you, the sweet angel…
Who sleeps on the moon

COLD FIRE

Cold fire, fire in your eyes
Power of love, in the flame you will rise
Time is your friend, unlocking every door
Of the gateway to your dreams
Of the desire for more
A state of absolute freedom
Shining through with the truth
Tunnels of permanent light
Future of everlasting youth
Touch every soul you meet
Until life is complete
Mission of believing in all
Any surprise you recall
Perfection in every small sense
Togetherness, the only real evidence
First your wife, and then the world
First the diamond, and then the pearls
Some things one just cannot measure
When you've earned her love, everything is a treasure
Maybe you can't quite understand
But you can always find my hand
With passion you connect
All history you resurrect
You are what we know as the earth
The love, the power, the meaning…your birth
Every star in the sky is your light, is your worth

SUPREME BEINGS

This love, this pain, this hunger,
This anxiousness, this desire, this energy
I feel it consuming me and I want it even more
I want you, I want to become the world
This source is the center of the universe
Cast it out of its shadow
Set it into the light
Extract it from your gleaming eyes
And let love reign supreme
No, not a dream...a being supreme

SHADOWS

I've been to the inside
But still I know where my heart resides
I've been to the innermost
But still I've yet found no ghost
I've been to the other side
No shadow from which I'll hide
I've heard all the accolades
And I know all the colors, and all their shades
I've felt all the power
No, no pain can be too sour
I know who I am
I can weigh myself gram by gram
And I do not ask why
Because I've looked into your eye

AND IT ENDED IN SUNSHINE…

My head is guided by my heart
My mind is guided by my dreams
So nothing will ever
Appear as it seems

I never know, which direction I'll turn
I never know, which things I will learn
I never know, if the sun will burn

I come from very far away
I'm not from 'round here
But the images in my head
Come to me crystal clear

I take photographs of life
Instants of joy
I place them in my heart
And let love employ

Certain memories I own
Have never left my surroundings
And my life continues
To hang by those strings

I feel as though
I'm guided by the sun
And somehow, some way
It has made me the one

To reveal the treasures
That the world desires
And bathe in the waters
That quenches those fires

From the bottom of my heart
As the world's wind swirls
I'm waiting for a miracle
Tracing the oceans for pearls

These gems that I find
I only wish to share
With all of the people
Everyone, everywhere

So that they may absorb it
The warm sun on their shoulder
So that they enter orbit
Renew youth in growing older

Make a long lost friend
Of "ole' Father Time"
Make a message to send
Of "another mountain to climb"

Over whose peak
Resides a glowing light
Of an ancient garden
Of a mythical height

A place so high
It faded out of sight
To those who can't imagine
Actually taking flight

But it somehow lingers
Back to their birth
It runs through their fingers
It came from the earth

Something pertaining
To mother's milk
Something remaining
Smoother than silk

Lives inside you
Lives inside us all
From age eighty-two
To when you started to crawl

What is it?
It's been asked before
So hard to unlock
The key to this door

Enchanted, she always cried
She could see it in my eyes
Every time I lied

And she swam across
My every black night
Showed me the stars
That were once burning bright

She always knew
How did she know?
The sky is true blue
White is the snow

And so is the dove
So is the swan
But without love
They both will be gone

This is what she taught me
With her heavenly smile
Sailed out to sea
To show me the child

Living in every soul
At every end of the earth
From North to South Pole
That is our worth

Spellbound, she always sang
She was the one answering
Every time my phone rang

Now I sit thinking
At every sunset
As I watch the sun sinking
I have not found it yet

I remain there hoping…
Until the sunrise
Picturing her eyes
Wondering about the disguise

'Till I remember her voice
Telling me "it's no trick
You really have no choice,
It's not love that makes you sick"

Ah yes…
When I finally understood
I could truly see
What it means to be good

And still to this day
I see her beautiful face
And I still hear her say
With her infinite grace

"Now that you feel me,
You have read every sign,
What's yours is what's mine,
And it ended in sunshine…"